REFLECTIONS OF *Life*

E. BARRETT LA MONT

Copyright © 2023 E. Barrett La Mont. All rights reserved.

No part of this book may be reproduced, stored, or transmitted by any means—whether auditory, graphic, mechanical, or electronic—without written permission of both publisher and author, except in the case of brief excerpts used in critical articles and reviews. Unauthorized reproduction of any part of this work is illegal and is punishable by law.

ISBN: 979-8-88640-986-4 (sc)
ISBN: 979-8-88640-987-1 (hc)
ISBN: 979-8-88640-988-8 (e)

Because of the dynamic nature of the Internet, any web addresses or links contained in this book may have changed since publication and may no longer be valid. The views expressed in this work are solely those of the author and do not necessarily reflect the views of the publisher, and the publisher hereby disclaims any responsibility for them.

THE EWINGS PUBLISHING

One Galleria Blvd., Suite 1900, Metairie, LA 70001
1-888-421-2397

Contents

My Heart 1
My Friend 2
May I Take the Path to Your Heart 3
Loving You 4
Love is Addictive 5
Love Is 6
Live For Today 7
Life's Tenuous Journey 8
Life's Rainbows 9
Life is a Gift 10
I Wish I Had Seen the Child in You 11
I Wish I Had. 12
I Will Never Hear Your Voice Again 13
I Was Naked 14
I Once Loved 15
I Had A Dream 16
I Died Too 17
I Didn't Know 18
I Am What I Am 19
I Am So Blessed 20
How Precious is the Love 21
How Long Will I Live? 22
How I Long to be With You Once More 23
Houses 24
Finding 25
Farewell My Dreams 26
Drowning in the Sea 27
Drifting Off Into My Dreams 28
Do I Love You? 29
As My Days Grow Shorter 30
And You Are There 31

An Indian Summer Night	32
I Love You	33
We Never	34
We Found Love	35
We Once Met	36
What Are Children?	37
What Morning Brings	38
What You Bring Into My Life	39
Two People	40
Transformed	41
Through all Seasons of Love so True	42
Thinking	43
The Way You Love Me at Night	44
The Things that Touch our Hearts	45
The Little Boy	46
The Jewel of Crown Point	47
The Beauty of Old Glory	48
Someone Like You	49
Someone	50
Sailing at Full Sail	51
Reasons For Crying	52
Rosebud	53
Rapture of Love	54
Part of Your Life	55
Pain	56
Oh, Dear Mother of Mine	57
My Wife... My Hero	58
Never Give Up On Love	59

My Heart

When I gave you my heart I was afraid you would ask me to take it back... but you said that I was already a part of your heart.

I love you so.

My Friend

How many times in today's world do you meet someone
you can truly call your friend?

Someone that asks nothing. . .
but gives everything. . .
a person that by their presence in the room
can brighten up your whole day. . .

I have met such a person in you!

Being human and having the basic human desires. . .
there are many things I could ask of you. . .
but all I ask is that you continue to be as you are. . .
my friend!

May I Take the Path to Your Heart

O that I could take the path to your heart. . .
so our hearts could beat as one. . .

Let me lie at your side. . .
let me by your shadows shadow. . .

I want to hold you near. . .
just for a lifetime. . .
would that be long enough for you?

You will forever embrace my heart. . .
with just a glance in my direction. . .

Our time on earth is but a shadow. . .
moving in the night.

Loving You

My dearest one... you are all my beginnings... all my ends.
You're a lifetime of the warm summer sun rising on the brink
of all life's rainbows...

You are all my sunsets bowing ever so slowly
to the lovely kiss of the moon's magic light...

All of my hopes and dreams came full bloom in my life...
since we first met...

I have never felt such unbridled joy...

The need to be near you is a narcotic...
 that I cannot get enough of...

I feel your eyes reach out and touch my body...
your eyes that speak of love and whisper the words you want me to hear...
Forces far beyond you and I brought us together...
at this time and place.

Others can play hide and seek...
but we're home free!

Love is Addictive

Love is the most addictive drug we will ever experience. . .
It is the one thing that everyone wants to have. . .

Love can be a bright star. . . that engulfs our life. . .
with all of the sun's life-giving rays. . .
causing our life to bloom. . .

Love can be a bright star. . . that engulfs our life. . .
with all of the sun's life-giving rays. . .
causing our life to bloom. . .

Love can disguise itself and become the sunset that is
the beginning of our darkest night. . .
a night that introduces us to our shadows. . .
hidden in the black bowels of dreams gone astray . . .
(these are what we fear most, giving into love). . .

Love can raise us up to heaven or deliver us
 down to a lonely hell. . .

Given the choice we most often choose loves
sweet embrace and tender kiss. . .

For like an addict we will always return to loves
chance to bloom again!

Love Is

Love is being there when you are needed...
Love is being open enough to let the one you love give their
Love in return...
Love is always having the time...
not only to say what's on your mind...
but to listen to what is on their mind...
Love is sacrificing time so the one you love knows
you gave up something for them...
Love is being gentle... not only physically... but mentally too...
Let them win life's little battles and you will end up winning the war...
Love is doing the unexpected...
Love is making someone feel good about themselves...
At night never let the last word from your mouth be a word
said in anger...
Never!...
Love is giving them something they could never give themselves...
you!

Live For Today

Live for today. . .
don't dwell in the past. . .
But follow your dreams!

Life's Tenuous Journey

In the big scheme of things. . .
life is but a light that flickers
in the dark. . .
(a candle in the wind).

Having you for one moment. . .
brought more light than I could ever have expected. . .

I have been truly blessed. . .

You are the sunlight that nourished me and showed me the way on this tenuous journey. . . called life.

Life's Rainbows

You are the colors of all life's rainbows. . . you transcend
The darkest clouds. . . bringing joy and light into every corner
Of my being.

Life is a Gift

Life is our most precious gift from God. . .
Never take this journey frivolously. . .
Search for knowledge. . .
And never be afraid to give love. . .
For with knowledge and love. . .
we find the meaning of God's precious gift!

I Wish I Had Seen the Child in You

You must have been an precious and adorable baby. . .

And as you were growing up did you laugh a lot and cry tears of joy. . .

What were your first words. . .

Were you a good child. . .

Did you like school and what was your favorite subject?

Did you enjoy your first kiss?

Do you like to know when we kiss?

What are you afraid of?

Do I ever make you sad, and if so. . . do I comfort you?

Whatever the case, you are an adorable baby. . . now!

I Wish I Had. . .

Looking back on my life there are many things I would do over again. . .
or in another way.

I wish I had taken more time to hold more babies. . .
rock them to sleep. . . watch their eyes learn to follow you. . .
to smell their scent and hear their cue.

I wish I had hiked more trails. . .
fished more streams and seen more sunsets.

When I was young I wish I had taken the time to listen to the elderly. . .
for they have so much to give with all their wisdom.

I wish I had listened to my family more, instead of watching TV.
We may have all enjoyed those years more.

I wish I had followed my own heart. . . .
instead of doing what others thought I should do.

I wish I had shown more love to those that love me and with passion!

And last, but not least, I wish I had loved myself more, for then
I could have given it out more freely and more often!

I have found that you must love yourself to be able to love others.

I Will Never Hear Your Voice Again

You are gone and I will never hear your voice again. . .
or your soft touch.
I will grow accustomed to not having you around. . .

I hope someday you will forgive me for all the pain that I may have brought to your life. . .

What does one say to that special person that may have given me the joy I needed. . .

For indeed my whole being with you has always given me joy!

I Was Naked

When I came to you I was naked...
You dressed me in love...
compassion and kindness.
Now when I stand in front of a mirror (which Is you)...
the reflection I see... is that of me...
a better person now... for having known you.

I Once Loved

I once loved you from afar...

Now I just love you!

E. Barrett La Mont

I Had A Dream

I had a dream as a small child that Santa Claus would come and there would be wonderful toys around the Christmas tree. . .

I had a dream that I would start school. . .
and I would be afraid of things to come. . .

And somehow I made it through and along the way I made friends and found something called self-confidence. . .

I had a dream that I felt love for the first time. . .
my parents called it puppy love. . . .
and it made me feel grand. . .

I had a dream that the time had come for me to make my own way in life. . . and so I did. . .

I had a dream that there was a reward for working hard, being honest and living a good life. . .

You were my reward. . . and the love of my life!

I Died Too

When you passed away I felt as if I had died too.
All I could think about was when we would walk
that road we loved so much.
We always seemed to arrive in time to see
the deer jump the fence heading down to the creek.
As we walked back to the cabin the sun would be setting over
the Sierra Nevada Mountains.

Life was new. . . even though we had been together for years.
When I found out you were going to leave this life I never
once gave up on your and I knew I would stand by your side
until your last breath.

Thank you for all that you gave me, for all those years.

I Didn't Know

I didn't know I was searching for you. . .
until you found me.

I Am What I Am

I am what I am. . . no more or no less. . .

I am the sum total of everything that came before. . .

I was born unflawed. . .

I have been molded from what is good and what was bad. . .

I am all the love that was generously given me. . .

I inherited my prejudices. . . I did not ask for them. . .

In the end I am what I am. . .

Please don't expect me to be what you want me to be. . .

Accept me for what I am!

I Am So Blessed

I am so blessed that I am the recipient of your love...

A love that has no boundaries or conditions...

You manage to raise me up with just a word...
a look...
a touch...

You give me wings to fly to new heights...

You have synced my mind with my heart...
creating a wondrous warm feeling in my soul...

I love what you have made of me...
I am so much better off, for the privilege of knowing your love...

Thank you for your endearing soft and gently ways...

I have only to look into your beautiful eyes to feel loved!

How Precious is the Love

How precious is the love. . .
That awakens me by the light of morn. . .
You are the sunshine. . .
Only you can bring light to my day. . .
Your gentleness brings warmth to my soul.

I shall live all my days. . .
With the taste of your love on my lips. . .
I am nourished by your loving voice. . .
My forever may last another day or another decade. . .
But my love for you is endless and will never die.

How Long Will I Live?

How long will I live. . .
long enough to see you have a good life. . .
And my children grown and happy. . .
To see the mountains change from year to year. . .
with their beautiful seasons and colors. . .
To watch the beautiful salmon do their love dance up the streams. . .
knowing they will be back next year. . .
I know I have never loved you more than I do right now.

How I Long to be With You Once More

I remember the day you were born. . . I didn't view your birth but I was over to the viewing room as fast as I could be. . .

I knew you the second I saw you. . . you were so cute. . .
so soft and cuddly. . . my eyes followed your every movement. . .

I was so proud to have this wonderful little gift from God. . .
I wanted to show you off to everyone. . .

You were so easy to love and care for. . .

Thank you for coming into my life and changing it forever.

Houses

Houses are built with wood, stucco and concrete.

Homes are built with love!

Finding

Finding is the reward for having searched.

Farewell My Dreams

Farewell my dreams...
My heart...
My soul...

Farewell to love... goodbye to everything that is meaningful...
My heart... my soul... and thoughts that gave them to me.

Drowning in the Sea

I was drowning in the sea of love. . . when you came to my rescue.
You asked me to take ahold of your heart. . . as I reached out
To embrace your heart I felt your strength and love engulf my body.
I no longer was afraid of drowning. . .
I was saved by your warm and loving embrace.

Drifting Off Into My Dreams

Sometimes just between being in the real world and
drifting off into a dream. . .
I have wonderful thoughts about you. . .

In these moments of semi-consciousness, I think of you and how I wish
that I had more of these precious moments. . .
moments gone for now. . .
but never completely forgotten. . .

I wish I had held you just one more time and told you how truly dear
you are to me. For you are the sun which brightens my day and the
stars that I turn to. . . when daylight is no more. . .

You bring the world to life and everything in it is better. . .
for having you in my world. . .

I hope that you will overlook my many faults and forgive them. . .
Without your enduring love. . . my life would be a empty void. . .
I love you with all my heart and what you bring to my world.

Do I Love You?

You ask me "do I love you"... well my darling... at my age...
and being on the shorter side of life...
I feel compelled to answer you most directly...
I can't think of anything or anyone that is dearer to me...
every day is precious... more precious than gold...
And with you at my side every second of every day is important...
God gives us all a definite time here on earth...
We must choose wisely who we spend time with...
I am so happy that I was smart enough to have chosen you...
I'm not saying that I made it easy for myself...
For a life worth having you, you must pay a price...
I would pay that price ten times over... just to be near you...
On our worst day... life is so much worth the price I pay...
to be at your side...
You have made me feel complete as a man and a human being...
You rock my boat... ring my chimes...
and keep me on the straight and narrow...
To make a long story short... YES I DO LOVE YOU!...
I thank God every day for the honor of having you for a lifetime!

As My Days Grow Shorter

As my days grow shorter and my end draws near. . .
there might be things in my life I would consider changing. . .

But having the honor of loving you is not one of them!

And You Are There

When alone with my thoughts... and all others have forsaken
Me... I just think of you... and you are there...

When I am down... destroyed by a mean word... and the world
Is a lonely place... I think of you... and you are there...

Your love is a part of my total being... for no matter where I am...
No matter what my life may have in store... I just think of you...
And you are there...

I will hold you near to my heart... until forever is no more...
I will be by your side... when your laughter embraces me...
And I will be there to share your tears on rainy days...
Just think of me... and I'll be there.

An Indian Summer Night

As the evening winds its way into the night. . . the last silky clouds
make their way across the Indian summer sky.

Accented by the shadows of blue found in babies eyes. . .
they form patterns as cream being poured on freshly
brewed coffee on a cold Winters morning.

The trees begin to sing their lullaby to the coming of night. . .
and quickly the birds find a resting place above. . .
as the creatures below in unison do the same.

As the moon peeks its face over the indigo mountains
shining light on all those below. . .
The world rests and awaits a new day!

I Love You

I want to say I love you. . .
To reach out and touch your hand, but also to hold your heart.

To be so close, each breath is a whisper,
and each whisper would tell of my love for you.

To know the feelings of your tenderness. . .
and the joy of living to love you alone. . .

Then being grateful for each day I can be awakened by the words that mean so much.

I love you.

We Never

We never kissed.

We never held hands.

We never made love.

Where did we connect?

Our hearts touched . . .
and for a moment. . .
we were one!

We Found Love

We found love in a world just like this one. . .
but void of love. . .
until we met.

We Once Met

We once met on a path traveled by only those that are
Destined to find one another. . .
By an accident we call fate!

What Are Children?

Children are the mirror that leads us down the path to our youth.

What Morning Brings

Sometimes I wake up before dawn... and I think of you...
Even in the dark... I can see your lovely face there beside me...
As the night turns into the soft light hours of morning...
turning over in bed... I behold your dear face...
and I know I'm waking up to another day of life...
but just as important to me...
I wake up with your there in it.

What You Bring Into My Life

Sometimes just between being in the real world and drifting
off into a dream I have wonderful thoughts about you.
In these moments of semi-consciousness I think of you and
how I wish that I had more of these precious moments.
Moments gone for now but never completely forgotten. . .
I wish I had held you just once more time and told you how
truly dear you are to me. . . for you are the sun that brightens
my day and the stars that I turn to when daylight is no more.
You bring the world to life and everything in it is better for
having known you. I hope that you will overlook my many
faults and forgive them. Without your enduring love my
life would be an empty void. I love you with all my heart
and what you bring into my life.

Two People

We were two people living different lives
in separate worlds. . .

Brought together by an unforeseen love that would bond us together. . .
until time was no more.

Transformed

I once was an awkward caterpillar that turned into a bashful cocoon and later became a beautiful butterfly.

Through all Seasons of Love so True

Through all the seasons of love so true... the winter... fall... spring and summer too... no greater love was felt in my heart... than the love I felt when we did part...

That was a time when my darkest night became my darkest day and the deepest winter felt like it was here to stay.

I had loved only you and now you are gone and I was left with a life that felt empty... I was all alone... with no one to turn to and nowhere to run...

Thinking

There are those that think solely with their hearts. . .
and those that use their minds. . .
but it takes both. . . to understand.

The Way You Love Me at Night

When the dark of night creeps into our room and you join me for
a nights rest, wonderful things happen to me, all because of you.

As I am laying there and dreaming of joyous things, I feel your touch.
Ever so gently I feel you soft fingers caress my neck and shoulders.
I can feel your eyes taking in every part of my face and you are there,
just as much as if we had never said "good-night."
I never say a word, but hear every word, the words you whisper
come from words left unsaid in your heart.

Your eyes and your hands say everything and you never realized
I was aware of one spoken word.

The Things that Touch our Hearts

The things that touch our hearts are the things
that give us the most pleasure. . .
The same things that we remember forever. . .
The things we look forward to seeing again. . .
The things we enjoy giving to others to see their faces light up. . .
Without them life means a little less. . .
To have your heart touched you must reach out to others and touch them!

The Little Boy

I know a little boy, who is with me every day. I am not always aware of him, but he is there anyway. He's a wonderful little child and I do love him so, but I don't always pay attention to him, why I do not know.

I see him in the things I love, his bright, inquisitive eyes. His ability to laugh at almost anything, and he totally lets go when he cries.

It's this same little boy who makes me laugh and play, sending me to the moon, even on my darkest days. I tell him that I'm here for him and he loves me so. He tells me everything will turn out fine, I'll never let him go.

I try to ease his mind, when life seems to have lost control. . .
I tell him not to blame himself, he is such a gentle soul.

He can't be held responsible for others uncaring ways. . .
he should love himself for what he is and not listen to what others might say. I feel our relationship is all that it should be. He makes me feel like a child again. . . and that means the world to me, I try to give him what he has never before received. . . and hold him to my heart with all the love he needs.

We shall talk of things we've never done and that I hope we'll never part, the best of our relationship, and this I truly mean, is the little boy, whom I hold dear, is the other side of me.

The Jewel of Crown Point

By dawn's early light it majestically touches the morning sky...
in the evening it reaches up so tenderly... embracing the stars...
then kisses the day goodbye...

It's a symbol of our beautiful state and those that came before...
It welcomes weary travelers... and with open arms we share a ride
through space and time... to a place that is no more.

Below it lies the Columbia River and the Cascade Mountains high...
Stretched out as far as man can see... a present from up above...
It's a home for you and me.

Treasure this special gift... nurture it so tenderly... we are the
caretakers of "Vista House"... a place for all to see... may our love
for this monument be everlasting and long endure...
and shine its light on thee!

The Beauty of Old Glory

On the Fourth of July in the heat of the day we look up to the sky and remember another time when men had to fight and die. . .
They died to make our nation free and all good men standing tall, for isn't that what it was all about in this greatest land of all?

Their blood that spilled onto the ground was given to make us free and we should be proud and see our flag there waving for all to come and see. . . that this land was made for everyone. . . let us hear for the red, white and blue. long live America for all eternity!

Someone Like You

When we were living in a younger world you walked into my life.
Things happened slowly and we both matured. . .
Then by some tiny twist of fate. . . we each went our different ways. . .
But even as you were gone. . . I knew I would always have to
have "someone like you" to make me feel complete. . .
As my life went on. . . I searched for "someone just like you"
Until I realized that I couldn't fine "someone just like you"
There is no one just like you!
So with that thought in mind. . . I set out to find you. . .
Well. . . long story short. . . I found you and never did settle
for "someone just like you". . . ! got you!
Moral. . . never settle for something second best. . .
be true to yourself. . . always take the best!

Someone

Someone that can listen to negativity. . .
but cannot be controlled by it. . .

Someone that knows all my faults and loves me anyway. . .

Someone that looks to the clouds on a rainy day and thanks God for another day of life.

And on-the last day of their life. . . someone that can look into the mirror and say. . . I lived life to its fullest.

Sailing at Full Sail

I took the helm and headed straight with my sails open and bellowing. . . straight for the horizon. . .
It was a love affair with me at the helm. . . the sea and the wind were blowing. . . blowing my heart. . .
I put the spinnaker out and felt its magic catch the boat and away we went. . .
It was like gliding on air. . .
Unlike anything I had ever felt. . .
As we went into every wave my love with the sea nourished my passion. . . I fell deeper in love with every wave that kissed the bow. . .
I had taken on her challenge. . . as she had taken on mine. . .
And I knew that we would be companions forever.

Reasons For Crying

We cry to forget...

We cry for remembering...

And we cry to help mend a broken heart...

Whatever the reason... it's a good thing!

Rosebud

As the dormant rosebud reaches up to the sun for new life
in the spring. . . so do I reach out to you for your warmth.

You are my spring and my light. . . just as the sun that touches
the rosebud to make it bloom. . . your light engulfs me and
I too have blossomed. . .

Like the blossoming rose I am fragile. . . but don't hold your
tears on cloudy days or in your brightest moments. . .
let them fall freely and nourish my roots.

The rose does not run the spring shower or a heavy downpour. . .
For it is the same moisture that both nourishes it and gives it life.

I will be there to catch your tears of joy. . . I shall be there to
sooth your tears and pain. . .

As with the union of the rose and sunshine. . . the day may
come when the petals wither and die. . . but grieve not for
the rose. . . for it has seen the beauty of spring. . . and has had
it's day in the sun.

Rapture of Love

In winter hold my hand and keep me warm. . .
for if you will do that to me I shall hold you dear to my heart.
In the fall let the gentle mist that blows off the ocean
touch down on your skin and soften it. . .
In the summer let your soft skin turn brown and
your eyes be the thing that gives me warmth. . .
In spring feel the new life bringing all hearts
together to love in a mighty rapture of love.

Part of Your Life

I don't want to be part of your life. . .
I want to be part of every breath you take.

I want to hold your soul in my hands.

I want to see the world as you see it and touch your heart. . .
as you touch mine.

Pain

The deepest and most devastating pain is never seen. . .
it hides in our hearts.

Oh, Dear Mother of Mine

You are the one that gave up everything to make my life the best it could possibly be.

You sacrificed much of your precious time to see that I had unconditional love.

You were my teacher and confidant. . . . you gave meaning to each day of my life and showed what unconditional love really was.

I may not have understood the meaning of what you were saying at that moment. . . but I understood the love in your eyes was the most important gift you had to give.

You loved me down to the core of my being. you truly gave the gift that endures forever.

My biggest regret was not being able to thank you for your enduring legacy of love. . . and how your legacy has enriched my life.

You are in my heart and will be there until I am no more.

My Wife... My Hero

You have been and will continue to be my hero...
I wish I were more like you.
Your strength is the glue that binds us together...
No matter how far I fall... your wisdom and guidance light up my day.
You have a healing and nurturing way that is there always...
Not bigger than life... you are my life... and when our lives on
earth are through and it's time to pass on to another dimension...
I pray God takes me first... without my hero life would be a
meaningless series of minutes... hours... days... and years.
Everyone needs a hero... to look up to... to emulate... and admire...
You're all these things... and will always continue to be until time
has passed us by.

Never Give Up On Love

Never give up on love. . . for if it finds you worthy. . .
it will never give up on you.

Love. . . like hope. Will live eternal!

www.ingramcontent.com/pod-product-compliance
Lightning Source LLC
LaVergne TN
LVHW041635070526
838199LV00052B/3373